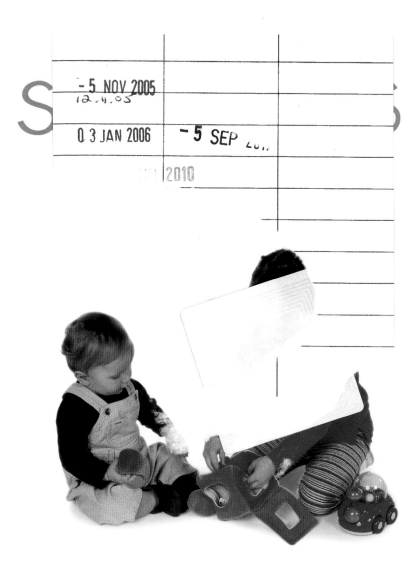

siblings

encouraging your
children to be friends

Dr Richard C. Woolfson

hamlyn

649.143

contents

First published in Great Britain in 2003 by Hamlyn, a division of Octopus Publishing Group Ltd 2–4 Heron Quays, London E14 4JP

Copyright © Octopus Publishing Group Ltd 2003

Distributed in the United States and Canada by Sterling Publishing Co., Inc. 387 Park Avenue South, New York, NY 10016-8810

ISBN 0 600 60663 5

A CIP catalogue record for this book is available from the British Library

Printed and bound in China

10 9 8 7 6 5 4 3 2 1

Introduction

We all have memories from our own childhood, memories about brothers and sisters. Maybe you recall incidents when your older brother annoyed you by taking your favourite toy without asking. Perhaps you remember that wonderful summer you spent with your sister, playing lots of exciting games together.

'I remember one time when I was seven. I fell and cut my knee and my brother comforted me, put a plaster on the cut and gave me one of his sweets to cheer me up. I would love my children to care for each other that way.'

Barbara, mother of Anita (4) and Stephen (2)

Left Encouraging your children to play with each other from a young age will help lay the foundations for a positive sibling relationship.

Alternatively, it could be that you were an only child, convinced either that others who had brothers and sisters were much better off than you, or that you were more fortunate than them because you were the centre of attention at home! There is no doubt that sibling relationships are extremely important.

If difficulties between siblings remain unresolved during the childhood years, they can continue throughout adulthood. That's why you need to get your children off on the right foot together from the very start. This book is designed to help you achieve this goal.

On the other hand, brothers and sisters can enjoy a very special relationship – one that lasts through thick and thin, and stands the test of time. Yet this doesn't happen by chance. It depends on many factors, including their personalities and interests, but it also depends on the way you help them to get along with each other. What you do to guide and support your children matters.

This book is packed to the brim with advice on managing your children: how to deal with their fights and competitiveness; how to help them develop their

individual strengths; how to make each of them feel very special; how to encourage them to be best friends with one another. It will enable you to become more effective in ensuring that your children thrive together and enjoy each other's company.

***Above** After their parents, siblings are the most important people in a child's life.*

7

your
next baby

1

- Is there a right time?

- The second time is different

- Birth order and personality

- When it's your third or fourth

Is there a right time?

Some parents plan their second pregnancy as carefully as possible, although this is not an exact science! Others find the news that the second baby is on the way a bit of a shock.

Below Spending time together as a family will help to strengthen relationships between siblings.

When thinking about the best time to have a second (or third, or fourth) baby, consider the following practicalities:

- **There is no 'right' time that suits everyone.** The timing that suited your best friend might not be right for you.
- **There is no 'right' age gap.** Every gap between children has both advantages and disadvantages.
- **Your first-born doesn't 'need' a friend.** He has friends his own age, and you cannot be sure that your children will be pals anyway.
- **You may have to adjust your living space.** Depending on the size of your house, you may want a bigger family home.
- **Children are expensive.** Apart from food and clothes, there may be childcare fees to consider.
- **Your first child's personality.** If she is especially demanding, you could find coping with two small children extremely stressful.
- **Stage of development.** Some parents like to know that their older child is at nursery or school before the second one comes along.

How to decide

When trying to decide whether or not to have a second baby, ask yourself these questions:

* Do I feel more confident in my skills as a parent?
* Have I learned a lot about parenting through raising my first baby?
* Am I making this decision jointly with my partner?
* Am I healthy, fit, and physically and emotionally ready to have another baby?
* Is this choice mine, without any undue pressure being placed on me?
* Do I really want to have more than one child right now?
* Can I cope financially with the cost of raising two or more children?
* Are suitable childcare arrangements available if I want to return to work?

Resist any pressure to have a second child when you are not ready for such a commitment. But if you do feel ready to increase the size of your family, good luck!

Above *A new baby will need a lot of time and attention, so make sure that you are ready for these demands.*

'When Jon was about a year old I felt strong both physically and emotionally. Rob and I knew this would be a good time to have our second child. We also thought a younger brother or sister would be good company for him.'

Danielle, mother of Jon (6) and Angie (4)

11

The second time is different

Having a baby is always different the second time around and there are good reasons why this is so. There are many factors to consider when preparing for the arrival of a new child in the family. It is important to consider how the baby will affect you, you partner and your first child and what new challenges you will be faced with.

How is it different?

- **You are different.** Maybe only a year or so has passed since your first baby arrived, but you are not the same person. You are older and more experienced.
- **Your family is different**. The first time around you didn't have another baby to look after at the same time. This time you'll have a young child and a baby to care for.
- **Your relationship is different.** The link between you and your partner may be just as strong as it was before your first baby was born, but it has changed.
- **Your finances are different**. The chances are that your income is lower now than it was before your first baby was born. In addition, two children cost more than one.

Physical factors

There are also physical factors that make a difference. For example, if it is only a short time since your first delivery your tummy muscles may not have regained their original strength, so the pregnancy may show earlier. On the other hand, having morning sickness during your first pregnancy doesn't necessarily mean you'll experience it again this time.

Below There are bound to be extra pressures the second time around, but you will have experience on your side.

Most mothers report a greater level of tiredness second time around than on the previous occasion. There are a number of reasons for this. For instance, you may still be experiencing unsettled nights with your first-born. You have the additional responsibility of looking after your first child while pregnant with your second. You are also older now and your stamina is reduced compared to the first time. That's why it is best to accept all offers of help so that you can rest as often as possible.

Bear in mind, too, that it can take your body at least nine months to return to its pre-pregnancy state. Many women have difficulty getting their figure back, which in turn can have an adverse effect on their self-esteem. Another common concern is that problems experienced the first time around, for example post-natal depression, may re-occur the next time.

Here are some guidelines for preparing yourself for your second pregnancy:
• Follow a healthy diet.
• Avoid smoking and alcohol.
• Take suitable exercise.
• Make the effort to organize an occasional night out for yourself and your partner.
• Try to make time for yourself, perhaps by swapping childcare with another mum for the afternoon.
• Meet with other mothers by joining a parent-and-toddler group.

Above Many older children adore their younger brothers and sisters and will play happily with them for hours.

Birth order and personality

Birth order (whether your child is first-born, second-born or later-born, a middle child, an only child, and so on) can have a significant effect on the development of her personal qualities, characteristics and abilities.

Top tips

Do your best to avoid making comparisons

You may be tempted to compare your younger child with her older brother, say, in order to encourage her to try harder. However, this strategy will always backfire. No child likes having their individual talents and skills compared to those of a brother or sister. Instead, let each of your children develop their individual personality.

Encourage each child's individuality

The fact that a child is first-born, say, does not mean that she will definitely have the characteristics associated with this particular family position. Much depends on the way others respond to her and on the individual experiences she has within the family.

Typical characteristics

- **First-born:** tends to be the brightest child in the family, gaining the highest achievements educationally, and is usually very serious-minded.
- **Second-born:** tends to be easy-going, less concerned with school success and more concerned with friendships. She prefers the unconventional.
- **Youngest child:** tends to be confident, and able to handle worries on her own without seeking help. She also knows how to get the most out of any situation in which she finds herself.
- **Only child:** relates better to older people than to her peers and seeks approval for her actions. She is likely to make a good leader.

Birth order affects your children in a number of ways. For example, your first-born has you all to herself, at least until the next one comes along. This undiluted attention from parents during the early years could be one reason why the typical first-born child is smarter than the others.

Then there is your own confidence as a parent. You learn a great deal about child-rearing through your experiences with your first-born – she is the family guinea pig, so to speak. By the time your second and third children come along, you feel a lot more relaxed about your parenting skills.

'We definitely see a huge difference in their personalities. Sean takes everything very seriously. He likes to follow the rules. Mandy is much more outgoing and boisterous. She would rather spend an afternoon painting and making things with clay than read a book.'

Adam, father of Sean (8) and Mandy (4)

Left *How your children interact will depend on their developing personalities, and will change over time.*

Right *Your children will have different interests: encourage them to pursue these so that each develops a sense of self-worth.*

When it's your third or fourth

Many parents don't stop at two. And when you have more than two children in your family, the dynamics and relationships can change significantly.

Safety in numbers

The advantages of having a large family (that is, with three or more children) include:

- **Constant company for the children.** With three or more at home, each child usually has at least one other sibling for company.
- **They learn from each other.** Your youngest child gains a great deal from observing his older siblings, watching how they play and how they talk to their friends.
- **Helping hands.** If you have a large family, the chances are that one of the older children will be there to lend a hand with a task involving the younger ones.
- **Accumulated experience.** You quickly build up your parenting skills with each successive child, enabling you to cope more effectively.

Of course, there are some potential disadvantages, too. For instance, there is the expense factor. Even with hand-me-down clothes in good condition, raising three or four children makes a big dent in the family budget. Holiday plans may need to be scaled down, eating out is a costly business with a large family, and it may be more difficult to visit or stay with friends and relatives. Then there are the time demands: four sets of parents' nights at school, four sets of leisure activities and four sets of homework can pose a logistical problem.

Below Younger children learn from their older siblings: find activities for them that they will both enjoy.

Personal choice

You have to decide what family size suits you best. When considering whether or not to expand your family beyond two children, try imagining scenarios like this:

- It's a sunny day and you have to take your four children on a journey to the park.
- You have to plan a family day out so that all your children are satisfied.
- Mealtime is approaching and your four children all have their own likes and dislikes.
- Your youngest child complains that you never buy him new clothes.

If these potential situations fill you with excitement, then a large family may suit you. If they fill you with dread, you may find that one or two children are enough for you.

Below A larger family will mean more work but, by your third child, you will be more confident in your skills as a parent.

Case study

When Jessica and Dave had their fourth child (the other three were nine, seven and three years old) they were extremely confident. Experience of bringing up their first three meant they had thrown away their parenting L-plates years ago. This didn't mean they got everything right, simply that they stopped worrying about the sorts of minor details that trouble first-time parents – such as the colour of the baby's bootees, or the noise that her rattle makes.

the new
baby arrives

2

Your vulnerable first-born

As far as you are concerned, you probably think that your older child's life goes on just as it did before your second child arrived. But she may not see it that way – and even if there are no actual changes to her normal routine as a result of the new arrival, she may be afraid that they will occur eventually.

Above The sound of a baby crying can be a cause of distress for an older sibling.

Like it or not, your first-born will be affected by her younger sibling's presence in the family, in a number of ways. For example:

- **Attention.** The fact is that you cannot give her as much attention as you did when she was the only child at home. Your new baby needs your care, which leaves you less time to spend with your older child.
- **Patience.** Looking after two children is tiring. You may find that you are more irritable and less patient – especially in the early weeks and months

– perhaps snapping a little too quickly at your first-born because of lack of sleep. You can't just take a nap when the baby does if you also have an active toddler to look after.

- **Routine.** It's not easy to continue with family life as it was before your second child was born. Those afternoon outings when it was just you and your child may have to be cancelled for a few months.
- **Noise.** Babies cry – that's how they communicate. But your older child could be distressed by this. It could be that the noise actually upsets her because she thinks the baby is upset, or perhaps the screaming interrupts and distracts her.

Forewarned

You'll be more sensitive to your older child's feelings – and more effective as a parent – when you anticipate the impact that the new arrival can have on her way of life. Try to see things from her point of view, so that you are sympathetic rather than critical, understanding instead of irritated. She will adjust to these changes at home in time, but it won't happen overnight. Give her your sole attention at some point every day and make sure she still feels special.

Case study

Fiona's parents hadn't given much thought to the effect that their new baby would have on her, and so they were quite surprised when this normally assertive and confident 3-year-old suddenly clung tightly to them, afraid to let them out of her sight. Moreover, whenever they gave the new baby attention Fiona would burst into tears, claiming that she had hurt herself or that she had lost her favourite toy.

Left Try to spend some 'baby-free' time with your older child every day, doing things that she enjoys.

Breaking the news

Naturally, you want your child to be excited about the prospect of a new addition to his family – and he could genuinely think the news is fabulous – but you should also expect him to be apprehensive and possibly angry. You can hardly blame him for being anxious at the thought of sharing you with someone else.

Right Letting your older child touch your pregnant tummy will help him get used to the idea of a new baby brother or sister.

Left Take time to explain to your child what is going to happen and reassure him if he is worried about anything.

Your first-born might not understand why you want to have a second child. In his young mind, he may be afraid that you will love the new baby more than him and that he will be less important to you. Of course this fear is silly as far as you are concerned, but it may be a very real worry for him, resulting in feelings of insecurity.

Top tips

Give advance notice

Tell your first-born child in advance that he is going to have a new brother or sister. Don't wait until the last moment, and don't tell him too soon, either – say, when you are only a few weeks into your pregnancy.

Timing matters

Start introducing the idea of the new baby when your tummy is large enough for him to notice. Be prepared to answer him when he asks you where the baby comes from.

Choose a suitable level

Pitch the conversation at a level suitable for his age and stage of understanding. For instance, you could say to your 4-year-old 'I've got a terrific surprise for you. We're going to have a new baby soon. I'm so excited.'

Anticipate reactions

Expect him to ask lots of questions – anything from 'Is the baby going to be a boy or a girl?' to 'Will the baby have to sleep in my bed with me?' Be ready for any reaction from him, so that you can respond appropriately.

Introduce him to other babies

He'll feel comfortable being around babies when he spends more time in their company. Try to take him to a baby-and-toddler group or to meetings with friends who have babies.

Let him feel your tummy

When your pregnancy is well advanced and you can actually feel your baby moving around, let your older child place his hand gently on your tummy so that he can feel the baby's activity, too. He will be very excited.

It's time to go!

You need to be organized for that moment when you go into hospital for the second delivery, whether labour starts right on time or catches you by surprise a few days earlier than expected. The same applies even if you choose to deliver your second and subsequent babies at home, which some women do after an uncomplicated first delivery in hospital.

Below Arrange for someone to care for your older child in your home while you are in hospital. This will help to minimize any anxiety.

Well in advance, explain to your child that when she was born you went into hospital to be cared for by the doctors and nurses, and that the same thing will happen with her younger brother or sister. Here are her most likely concerns:

- **Worry about herself.** She needs to be told clearly who will look after her while you are away – for instance, that her father or grandparent will be there for her. If possible, arrange for her to be in her own house while you are in hospital, rather than staying with someone else.
- **Worry about arrangements.** Your first-born wants her life to continue as normal while you are away, because this is very reassuring for her. Try to ensure that she continues to attend nursery each day, and that she is able to go to her usual mid-week gymnastics class, too.
- **Worry about you.** She's not used to being at home without you and she has probably never thought about you in relation to hospitals before. Make a good guess about how long you'll be in hospital, add an extra day to be on the safe side, and then tell her 'I'll be back home on Monday.'

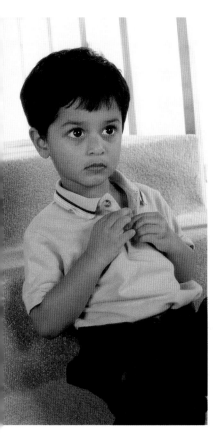

Above *Seeing you go through childbirth may frighten your older child but, on the other hand, being there to greet his new baby brother or sister can be exciting.*

Should she be there?

Many people have strong views about the suitability of having the older child present during the delivery of the new baby. In addition to planned home deliveries, there have been many instances where a baby was born at home because the mother did not have time to make it to the maternity hospital, meaning the older child observed the whole process. Parents who have been through that experience often comment how it brought the family closer together.

It is your decision whether or not your older child should be present at the second birth, along with the professionals who care for you. However, consider carefully the impact it could have. She may view the whole process positively; on the other hand, if she sees you in pain and discomfort during labour – even though you know this is a normal, natural experience – she could build up negative feelings towards the new arrival. Think this through before making up your mind.

The first meeting

The first meeting between your older child and your new baby needs to be handled sensitively. It is most likely that this very special occasion will occur while you are still in the maternity hospital. Everybody is a little anxious: your older child is apprehensive about his new sibling, you are desperate to see him, and your partner wants everybody to get on with each other.

Below *Getting an older child to make a gift or a card for the new baby will help him to feel more involved.*

Five golden rules

Here are five golden rules to ensure your children's relationship gets off to a great start:

1 Realistic expectations.
Unfamiliar hospital surroundings often confuse an anxious child, especially if he is very young, and he may appear to be remote and distant from you. His normally effusive personality may be subdued at this time, as he scans this strange environment very carefully. Do not be upset by this – he needs time to adjust. Instead of waiting for him to talk to you, give him a huge cuddle.

2 Attention.
Make your older child the centre of attention to start with – there is plenty of time for him to venture over to the baby. Ask him to tell you about all the things he has been doing while you have been in hospital. You will find that he gradually unwinds and will spontaneously ask questions about the new baby.

3 Gift exchange.
Tell your first-born that the baby has a new present for him, which is in the cot. Explain that the baby thinks he is a terrific big brother. Your child

will be delighted with this gift. Then hand him a small present that he can give to the new arrival. This very practical ceremony cements a positive relationship between the siblings.

Above *Let your older child approach the baby at his or her own speed and encourage gentle physical contact.*

4 Physical contact.
During this first contact, your older child will eventually drift over to the new baby – curiosity gets the better of him, despite any initial reservations. Relax: he won't do any harm to his young sibling just by stroking her face or touching her little fingers. He will be fascinated by the fact that she's so much smaller than him. Be prepared for some prodding and poking!

5 Answer questions.
Your child aged 3 or 4 years has the capacity to ask questions that you find difficult, such as 'Will that ugly mark on her face ever go away?' or 'Why is her head that funny shape?' Do your best to answer these remarks as calmly as you can. Try to strike a positive note, and do your best to conceal any tension you might feel.

sibling rivalry

- The age gap counts

- The facts about sibling rivalry

- Sibling rivalry:
  questions and answers

- How sibling rivalry shows

- Ages and stages (1 to 5 years)

The age gap counts

The age gap between your first and second children affects their relationship; it also affects you and your partner. Although every child, and every parent, is unique, findings from psychological research highlight common effects of different age gaps. There are also some practical repercussions on your daily life.

Less than 2 years

- There is a strong possibility your children will grow up to be good friends, especially when the younger child reaches school age.
- As your first child is still quite young when the baby is born, she is less likely to feel threatened by the new addition.
- You may not have recovered fully from any health difficulties you experienced as a result of the first birth, leaving you physically vulnerable.
- If you have taken time off from your career to raise your first child, having another baby so soon might have left you with no time re-establish yourself at work.

2 to 4 years

- Your older child's increased understanding means that she is more likely to feel annoyed with the new baby, and sibling rivalry may be stronger as a result of this.
- When you feed your baby, your first-born may feel jealous because she sees you both in such close physical contact.

Below Encourage your children to play with toys that they can use together – there is less likely to be any resentment.

Remember

These research results represent trends, not absolute certainties. Although they are informative, do not base your decision on the age gap between your children solely on these observations.

- Your first-born's daily schedule is different from the baby's routine – she stays up later and has her own friends, and this makes her feel like a special 'big sister'.
- As your older child has outgrown her baby toys and clothes, you won't have to buy so many new items for your second baby.

More than 4 years

- You have lots of time to spend with your new baby because your older child is at school all day during the week.
- Your older child can continue with her after-school activities despite the demands of her younger sibling. Arrangements can be made for her to get a lift from a friend's parents, for example.
- Your older child might want to show off about her family's new addition, perhaps by telling her classmates or teacher.
- You will need time to adjust to family life with a new baby, having now got used to your child being less dependent on you.

Above *Your older child may resent the close physical attention that your baby gets. Compensate with lots of cuddles and hugs for him, too.*

The facts about sibling rivalry

The origins of sibling rivalry – that is, jealousy between children of the same family – usually lie in the first 5 years of life. When your first-born child is knocked off his perch by the arrival of the new baby, the resentment and jealousy often starts. Whereas before the birth your older child had you all to himself, he now finds that the new baby takes up a lot of your time and attention.

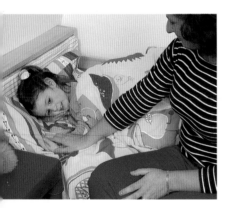

Above *Bedtime is a common cause of disagreement: explain to your younger child that she will be allowed to stay up later as she grows up.*

Psychological research shows that even second and third-born children can feel resentment towards a new baby. Younger children are likely to experience jealousy, too, especially when they think that older brothers and sisters are allowed more freedom, later bedtimes, or more new clothes.

When this form of jealousy does exist, it results at best in verbal disagreements between your children as they shout and even scream at each other, and at worst in raised hands as they try to thump each other. (Of course, you may be delighted to discover that your children actually have a trouble-free relationship.)

Other facts

Here are some other facts about sibling rivalry:

- Virtually every child can feel jealousy towards their sibling, depending on the circumstances – even your mild-mannered son or daughter can feel negative about their brothers and sisters at times.
- Sibling rivalry tends to be strongest when the youngest child is 3 or 4 years old. This means that having children aged, say, 3 and 5 years, may involve you in smoothing out frequent fights between them.

- Fist fights are more common than verbal disagreements when one of the children is around the age of 2 or 3 years. At this stage of development, a child is typically very quick to be physically aggressive towards his sibling.
- When siblings aged 3 or 4 argue with each other, the disagreement usually revolves around a game or toy. They both want to play with the same item at the same time and haven't yet developed a mature ability to share.
- When brothers and sisters aged 4 or 5 years engage in conflict, they are less concerned about accessing an object and more concerned with demonstrating their own power and influence.
- Every child is different. You might have one child who is extremely passive and is prepared to let his sister do what she wants, whereas your other child might be ready to pounce on his sister every time she does something he doesn't like.

Above *Young children are more likely to resort to pushing and shoving in squabbles over toys as they haven't yet developed the skills for sharing.*

Sibling rivalry:
questions and answers

Q Does every parent have children who fight with each other all the time, or is it just my children who are like this?

A Sibling rivalry is so common in families that most psychologists would regard it as normal. Speaking to your friends about their family life will confirm this to you. Logic dictates that when there is a limited amount of time and resources available, each child competes for his own share and, not surprisingly, this is a recipe for jealousy between them.

Q Why is it that their arguments usually start over trivial incidents, such as which television programme to watch or what game to play?

A So often these arguments appear to be straightforward and trivial, and yet typically they have a deeper, hidden agenda. For instance, the real cause of your children's fight may not simply be that they both want to play with same toy at the same time – rather, it could be that each wants to assert their territorial rights. It's often a matter of power, not possessions.

Q Why should knowing that others experience sibling rivalry too make any difference to me, as I still have to deal with it anyway?

A You may be inclined to blame yourself for the tension that occasionally arises between your

Above *When both children are old enough, simple board games are a good way of avoiding squabbles.*

children. There is a lot you can do to ease those pressures (and this book is full of advice and suggestions for achieving this target), but you are unlikely to be able to remove rivalry altogether. This knowledge should reduce any feelings of self-blame.

Above *Sharing small toys is another problem area – a younger child will not understand that his older sister wants to keep her toys to herself.*

Q My children don't fight with each other at all. Does this mean they are repressing their feelings of hostility towards their siblings?

A Not at all. Although rivalry is common, there are some children who never feel threatened or annoyed by the actions of their siblings. That's a very positive characteristic and clearly your own children come into this category. Instead of worrying about repression, relax and enjoy their trouble-free relationships.

Q Is there a certain age at which jealousy between children disappears altogether?

A There is no specific age at which this should stop. Many children do come to terms with feelings of sibling rivalry, either during childhood or towards the end of adolescence. In many instances, however, the jealousies and rivalries that existed during the childhood years are carried into adulthood – grown-up siblings can disagree, too!

How sibling rivalry shows

Every child is different and therefore the way in which sibling rivalry affects your child depends on his age, personality and stage of development. Here are some ways in which jealousy between brothers and sisters can show through, and some techniques you can use to tackle the situation:

Incident The minute you start to bath your 3-month-old baby, your 2-year-old toddler starts to whinge and roll around on the floor.

Strategy Make sure your toddler has something to do before you start bathing the baby. Give him a game or a toy to play with, or let him stay close to you so that he can watch you bath his younger sister. He is less likely to be attention-seeking when he is kept busy.

Below As your children get older, there will be more activities in which they can both participate.

Incident Your 2-year-old appears loving towards the new baby and yet he cuddles her so enthusiastically that she bursts out crying every time.

Strategy His mixed feelings of affection and apprehension are showing through in the form of an uncomfortable cuddle that actually causes distress to his sibling. Watch him closely at those moments and remind him to be gentle. Give him lots of praise when he plays appropriately with the baby.

Incident **Your 5-year-old shares a room with his 3-year-old sister but complains constantly that she plays on his side with his toys.**

Strategy Your child partly defines his role in terms of his personal space and personal possessions, and he wants this to be recognized. He resents his younger sibling's lack of respect. Explain to your 3-year-old the rules of asking permission before using her brother's toys.

Incident **At the end-of-year school concert, your non-musical 8-year-old is sarcastic about his younger sibling's musical performance.**

Strategy Your older child struggles to accept that his younger sibling could be more skilled in some ways than he is himself, hence his scornful remarks. Point out to your older child that he is talented, too, and that his young sibling looks up to him. Encourage him to be more supportive.

Incident **Although fully toilet-trained and dry during the day, your 3-year-old starts to wet himself soon after your second baby is born.**

Strategy Your child regresses to younger behaviour because he feels insecure. Don't get angry with him for wetting himself. Instead, give him lots of hugs and cuddles and make a special time for just you and him every single day.

Above *Encourage activities that your children can do together, especially if the older child can help the younger without seeming to take over.*

Ages and stages (1 to 5 years)

A child's personality develops significantly during the first 5 years and the tensions and stresses in sibling relationships change as the children grow older. Sibling rivalry is expressed differently depending on the age and stage of the children's development.

18 months

Your toddler is very egocentric and is not concerned with other people's feelings. She feels very powerful and she wants to be in control.

She is the older child

Sibling rivalry tends to be less severe because she is too focused on herself. She's happy as long as things don't change too much at home and she continues to receive affection.

She is the younger child

A toddler aged 18 months does not represent a great threat to her older siblings. However, she can still annoy them intensely!

2 years

She is probably full of her own self-importance. She wants everything to be done her way, otherwise she explodes in a tantrum.

She is the older child

She is smart enough to know that the new baby will have an effect on her life at home, and she may become attention-seeking and babyish as a result.

She is the younger child

Her curiosity forces her to explore and discover, much to the irritation of her older sibling who wants his privacy.

3 years

Being more independent, your child can do much more for herself. Her language has improved, too, so she is able to express her opinions clearly.

She is the older child
This age gap is associated with a high level of sibling rivalry. She knows that the baby will draw attention away from herself.

She is the younger child
Her older sibling expects her to follow the family rules, but she understands this and tries to cooperate.

4 years

Self-confidence has improved, and she mixes better with others her own age. Her sense of humour begins to show through.

She is the older child
She accepts the reality of the new arrival and she is less likely to be jealous at this age. At times, however, she can find her young sibling intrusive.

She is the younger child
She is extremely loyal to her older sibling, yet this can quickly turn to anger if she feels aggrieved or left out.

5 years

Starting school is a huge transition. She has a new and psychologically significant perception of herself as a 'big girl'.

She is the older child
She feels great about herself, and is often more tolerant of her young sibling. Occasionally, she tries to boss him about.

She is the younger child
Your child desperately wants to be like her older sibling, and she may feel hurt when he wants to play with his friend instead.

new baby
and toddler

- Home at last!

- Coping with more than one

- Toddler jealousy

- Encouraging kindness

- I matter, too

Home at last!

What a wonderful moment it is when you arrive back home with your new baby, safe and sound. Now you can get on with life as a two-child family. But things are different: your older child isn't used to sharing you with the baby.

Right Make sure that your older child feels that he is still just as important as before. Emphasize that she is his baby sister, too.

Playing his part

All that is required to help forge that vital connection between your older child and your new baby once you are back home is some thought, sensitivity and planning. Encourage all visitors to your house to bring a small gift for your older child. This gesture makes him feel that he benefits from the presence of his younger sister, too – that she's not the only one to get gifts. Of course, you can't always arrange this, but it is certainly worth a try.

In addition, make sure that these visitors spend a few minutes chatting to your older child before rushing off to meet the baby. Too often, vulnerable 2-year-olds are almost crushed unnoticed in the stampede to see the baby! A little bit of attention shown to him goes a long way

Remember that it's his new baby, too. Underlying all his mixed emotions at this early stage, he is still very proud of the new arrival and wants to show her off to anyone who is willing to listen. There is no reason why a child as young as 2 or 3 years should not lead friends and relatives to the baby's cot. A simple technique like this makes him feel very important.

Your older child watches you closely at this point, looking for signs that the baby is causing any disruptions to family life – his confidence is easily rocked in these early days after you return home from hospital. That's why you should do your best not to show irritation or stress in front of him, even though you may be exhausted and struggling with this new responsibility. If your older child sees that you are relaxed, you feels relaxed as well.

Case study

Charlie and Julie were thrilled with so many visitors to their home, all of whom wanted to see their lovely new arrival. Their 3-year-old, Danny, wasn't so thrilled, however. In fact, he was thoroughly miserable. Fed up with all the excitement directed towards his young sibling, he felt isolated and disconnected.

Above Encourage visitors to pay some attention to your older child as well as to your new baby.

43

Coping with more than one

Now that you are safely ensconced at home with your two (or more) young children – and the endless round of visitors has gradually faded away – it's time to get on with the wonderful business of raising them. However, there are a number of parenting challenges that become more prominent with two or more children.

Challenge 'I never have enough time to do everything.'

Strategy Do your best to plan your days, especially during the week. True, children and babies are unpredictable, forming their own schedule independent of any hopes you might have, yet some attempt at advance planning is better than none. For instance, plan that trip to your friend's house, even if you need two days of organization in order to make it. You need to get out and about once in a while.

Challenge 'I want to prove to myself that I can manage.'

Strategy Your confidence and self-esteem as a parent are vital, and it's only natural that you want to know you have the ability to be an effective parent. But you should also recognize that you have limitations. Nobody has unlimited supplies of energy and enthusiasm. Take help when it is offered, and ask for help if you need it. A little friendly assistance goes a long way.

Challenge 'One day is exactly the same as the next.'

Strategy One of the problems in caring for children under the age of 5 is that the routine of feeding, bathing and changing can quickly dominate, making every day seem the same. Don't lose sight of the terrific developmental changes that occur, as your new baby and young child steadily improve their skills. Keep them in focus.

Challenge 'I want to go back to work.'

Strategy If you want to return to work – whether part-time, job-sharing or full-time – you need to identify high-quality, reliable childcare arrangements. Consider all the options, such as day nursery or childminding, and calculate the likely cost of each alternative. Check out the availability of each well before you intend to return to work.

Above Childcare arrangements can provide the solution for a return to work and will also help your children to socialize.

Left Coping with the conflicting demands of two children, both of whom will want your attention every waking minute, can be exhausting.

Challenge 'I can't manage the housework as well as being a parent.'

Strategy Eliminate as many household chores as you can. You'll find that the world continues even though your house is less tidy than it was in the pre-children era of your life. If possible, leave a share of the domestic chores to your partner, or postpone them to a more suitable time, or ignore some of the trivial tasks altogether.

Toddler jealousy

The toddler era is often nick-named 'the terrible twos' because the typical child of this age wants everything done his way or else he screams blue murder – this is because he is truly egocentric, in that he literally sees the world only from his perspective.

Right Lots of reassurance should help to avoid temper tantrums inspired by jealousy. Try to understand how she's feeling, but don't give in to her.

Far right Sulking, uncooperativeness or even overt aggression can be signs of jealousy over the new arrival.

Top tips

The following suggestions will help you manage your toddler's jealousy:

Watch for the signs

You may be able to spot the early signs of jealousy when you know your toddler well enough. For instance, he might start to become irritable, or he might start to press himself against you as you try to feed the baby. If you recognize these signals, calm him before he becomes too upset.

Try distraction

Sometimes your child can be drawn out of the early stage of a jealous episode through distraction. Maybe he has a favourite toy or game, or perhaps there is a special book he likes. When you see him become agitated about his sibling, it's worth trying to distract him.

Reassure him

Whatever form his jealousy takes, talk to him in a calm and soothing voice, reassuring him that he is safe and that you and his sibling love him. Keep doing this until you feel that he has regained control of his emotions. You may find he then snuggles up to you and sobs.

The early years are dominated by two conflicting trends. First, your growing child has a deep need to form a close emotional connection with you and your partner. Second, he is desperate to become independent, to be able to do things for himself without your support. Add in the third ingredient – namely, jealousy of the new arrival – and you have a recipe for frequent tantrums.

Not all children show their feelings of insecurity in this way, though. Often, a child aged 2 or 3 years becomes possessive of his parents, or he may start to act in a babyish manner himself (for instance, by wanting to drink out of a bottle instead of an open cup, or by asking to wear a nappy during the day despite the fact that he is fully toilet trained). Some children become uncooperative or aggressive when feelings of sibling rivalry start to break through. It comes down to knowing your toddler and being aware of subtle changes in his behaviour that coincide with your baby's homecoming.

Encouraging kindness

Your toddler has an innate drive to be kind and considerate – this is hard to imagine sometimes, particularly when you see her stomping about in one of those rages!

How kindness develops:

- **1 week.** When your baby hears another baby cry, it is very likely that she will also burst into tears too because the other baby's distress makes her unhappy.
- **6 months.** She starts to giggle when she sees you giggle and starts to cry when she sees you cry.
- **1 year.** Your toddler grows worried when she sees someone else who is upset, but she doesn't yet think of going over to the other person to comfort them.
- **2 years.** When your child sees you carrying out a routine household chore, she tries to help in a genuine effort to support and assist you.

This inborn desire to care for and help others is present when your new baby is born. All your 2-year-old needs is some subtle guidance to turn these positive feelings towards her younger sibling as well.

She needs your help

You know, for instance, that a new baby is fragile, that he feels pain just like anyone else and that he can become frightened or confused. But your 2-year-old might not fully understand that. She's used to soft toys and life-like play figures that can be bashed about. So point out to her that her new sibling feels things in the same way she does. Explain that she should be gentle when touching or holding him.

Below If your toddler is a bit rough with the baby, it's unlikely to be deliberate; encourage her to be gentle.

She may want to show off in front of him, saying to you, for example, 'Tell my brother to watch me while I jump.' It may be clear to you that her baby brother has no awareness of what she is doing at that moment, but she wants him to admire her anyway. Help the process along by confirming that he saw her achievements and thought she was marvellous.

Getting your toddler involved in helping you with basic babycare chores such as washing, changing and so on helps her to develop a caring attitude towards the new arrival. However, don't force her to care. Practical actions like these enable her to see ways in which she can show kindness towards him. And if she wants to sing him a song at the same time, let her. To you, her singing might seem awful, but your baby probably genuinely enjoys it.

Above *Encourage your older child to play games with the baby and praise her when she does. The baby will enjoy it as well.*

I matter, too

Of course your toddler is special to you. The presence of another child in your family hasn't changed that in the slightest, but your vulnerable, insecure 2-year-old probably needs you to convince him of this fact. There are three main ways in which you can achieve this: first, by what you say; second, by what you do; and third, by what you change.

Above Reading a story together is a great way of giving your toddler the love and attention he needs.

What you say

Telling your toddler you love him makes him feel special. Naturally, he might not react with enthusiasm when you say this to him: he might carry on as if he didn't hear you, he might shrug his shoulders or he might even give you a glance of apparent disapproval. But don't be fooled – he delights in your positive remarks all the same.

Tell him how marvellous he is, how proud you are of him. In addition, reinforce the idea that his new sibling thinks highly of him. Your 2-year-old's self-esteem rises rapidly with the news that he is highly valued by his baby sister.

What you do

No matter how busy you are caring for more than one child at the same time, make sure you have time alone with your toddler every single day. The longer the better, of course, but even a few minutes is better than nothing at all. Use that time to chat with your 2-year-old, to play with him and to do things together.

Give him lots of cuddles and hugs. Watching you in close physical contact with your new baby can unsettle him. After all, he wants his fair share of that, too. He's certainly not too old for snuggling up against you while you read him a story, or for receiving a loving stroke of his hair.

What you change

Now that your toddler is the older child in the family, make some changes so that being the 'big brother' has certain rewards. For example, tell him that he can go to bed ten minutes later now that he's a 'big boy', or that he can use a different cup and plate now that he's older. This differentiates him from his younger sister, adding to his sense of importance.

Ask him to make minor choices regarding the care of your baby. For instance, he can choose the outfit for his sister to wear that day, or what toys she might like to play with in the bath that night.

Below *Spend time with your older child doing activities that she enjoys and give her lots of encouragement and praise.*

new baby and pre-school child

5

- Getting your child involved

- Attention-seeking: *questions and answers*

- Personal space

- Bickering and fighting

- There's too much going on

- Boosting self-confidence

Getting your child involved

While the typical toddler has an uninhibited enthusiasm for anything new – and that includes a young brother or sister – the typical pre-school child is more reserved. She has her own friends, her own games and her own likes and dislikes. This means that she may feel slightly distant from all the excitement surrounding the new arrival.

Below A pre-schooler is capable of taking on small responsibilities with his younger sister.

In addition, she is now old enough to realize that babies are fragile compared to her own age group: she knows that a baby is easily hurt and therefore she may be reluctant to become involved in looking after him, playing with him or holding him. Your pre-schooler is also keen to avoid doing anything that might upset you, which increases her apprehension about getting involved with her young sibling.

That's why it is a good idea to let your child hold your baby soon after they meet for the first time. Give her lots of advice so that she gets it right, though take care to avoid crowding her. The first time she holds him, make sure she is seated firmly on a chair with a supportive back. Bring the baby over to your child and nestle him in her arms. If persuasion is required in order to boost her confidence, tell her how delighted you are with her.

Significant responsibilities

Whereas you would only give a toddler minor responsibilities for babycare activities, you can reasonably expect your pre-schooler to play a more useful role. Here are some of the activities that she could take charge of:

- Pushing your baby alongside you as you all go out for a walk.
- Soothing him for a few minutes by gently rocking him back and forth.
- Playing with him for a short time with rattles and other suitable toys.
- Singing a song or reciting a nursery rhyme to him.
- Actively helping you with bathing and changing.

Under your supervision, these activities help bring your pre-schooler and the new arrival closer together – and as long as you are watching over them, nothing should go wrong.

Above Babycare activities such as bath-time can provide an opportunity for your toddler to interact with his baby sister.

'Jack was almost 4 when Chloe was born, and although he was mildly interested in her arrival he didn't show much enthusiasm for her once we were back home. He obviously thought that there wasn't much he could do.'

Amy, mother of Jack (4) and Chloe (1)

Attention-seeking:
questions and answers

Above *Ignoring a child's attention-seeking behaviour can be stressful, but it often works.*

Q Since our second baby was born, our 4-year-old has become very attention-seeking. Shouldn't he be past the stage where he can be affected in this way?

A Every child is different. Although your 4-year-old is mature in many ways, he remains emotionally vulnerable – the fact that he has become attention-seeking demonstrates this. It is very likely that the birth of his sibling has made him feel insecure. However, you should also check out other possible sources of stress – for instance, he may have fallen out with his best friend, or he may be more tired from adjusting to the long school day.

Q When he is attention-seeking (for instance, by talking loudly or showing off) we usually get angry with him. Why doesn't this stop his behaviour?

A As far as you are concerned, a loud reprimand in public should be an effective deterrent and so you expect your child to stop misbehaving when you show your annoyance with him. But he probably sees things differently. The moment you get angry with him, you give him your attention (negative attention, but attention all the same) and he would rather have this than see you give your attention to the new baby.

Q I have tried ignoring my 4-year-old when he is attention-seeking, but I find this very difficult because he creates such a fuss. Does ignoring a child work?

A Ignoring a child who displays attention-seeking behaviour is often a successful strategy. However, you need to be very determined to carry this out, and his behaviour could escalate to the point where you cannot ignore him any longer. The danger is that after ignoring your child for several minutes, you suddenly explode with rage. Once you have decided to ignore his behaviour, stick to your decision and try to control your temper.

Q What else can I do apart from ignoring him? I would prefer to take a more positive approach.

A As well as ignoring attention-seeking behaviour, give him attention when he does behave appropriately. For instance, praise your 4-year-old when you have been able to feed his baby sister without interruption, or give him a big hug when you are able to shop at the supermarket without him misbehaving. You can also reason with him, explaining why his good behaviour will be such a help to you. Maybe you can give him a little task to do while you are busy.

Above Letting your pre-schooler help with simple tasks like cooking is a good way of showing him that you think he's growing up.

Personal space

Life is usually hectic in a family with more than one child. And at times the children might feel they have no personal space, no room to themselves for some peace and quiet.

Problem Your 4-year-old is used to having her own room, but she now has to share it with her baby brother.

Solution When an older child cannot continue to have her own bedroom because accommodation is limited, resentment can build. Ease this situation by clearly marking out her 'side' of the room. Give her a bed, storage space, a desk or table at which to work, and a wardrobe. Keep all her items stored closely together.

Below If your toddler won't let her brother and his friends play in peace, you may need to distract her with a different activity in another room.

Problem Your baby cries during the night and your older child tells you that this upsets her and keeps her awake.

Solution Try to settle your baby to sleep before your older child goes to bed – let her stay up later if possible, until the baby sleeps. Reassure your 3-year-old that she'll soon get used to the sound, and that she will eventually sleep through without being woken. Or you might consider keeping your baby in your room until he sleeps through the night.

Problem Your older child complains that there is never any peace at home to watch television because her younger sibling usually disturbs her.

Solution Explain that family life involves give and take, and that everyone has to adjust to the others. In addition, however, suggest that she watches television when the baby is asleep, or that occasionally you will play with your baby in another room so that she won't be interrupted. Let her know that you want to help her.

Problem Your 4-year-old has become very secretive since your second baby was born, hiding her toys.

Solution The arrival of the baby has made her desire for privacy more intense, and hence she tries to conceal her possessions. This is her way of maintaining her personal space. Reassure your child that she doesn't have to hide her possessions in order to keep them safe. Explain that you will try to ensure nobody plays with her toys without her permission.

Above Persuade the older children to compromise; let them know that if they include the toddler in some activities, you'll make sure that they have some time to themselves, too.

Problem Every time your 5-year-old has friends over to your house, your toddler insists on playing with them, too.

Solution Whether or not your older child is fed up with the situation, do what you can to ensure that she and her pals have the freedom to play without interruption. Your toddler's excitement on seeing the older children (and his desire to be with his sister) is understandable, but your older child still needs her own space to be with her friends.

Bickering and fighting

Even with an age gap of 3 or 4 years between them, it won't be long before you hear your children bicker. When they do fight, despite all your previous warnings to play peacefully together, try to remain calm and resist the temptation to over-react. By all means let your children know that you are angry with them and explain that they should try not to argue, but also let them know that you still love them.

Above *Keep a close eye on games such as sword fights: excitement can easily tip over into aggression.*

It's never easy keeping discipline with two children of different ages – your younger one complains that his older sister is allowed to watch television later than he is and to go to bed later, too; your older one complains that you are too lenient with her young brother. You can't win!

Dealing with disagreements

There are several strategies that will help in sorting out your children's arguments and fights:

- Do your best to be even-handed. Your younger child isn't always the one who started the dispute, and your older one doesn't always push her little brother around.
- If they both present a plausible argument, be honest and tell them this – then act in a similar way towards both of them. That's all you can do. Bear in mind also that one child might become upset when his sibling is to be punished, even if she deserves it. This show of concern could make you reconsider the severity of the punishment.
- Try to anticipate potential flashpoints and then avoid them. For instance, if your younger child annoys your older one when she has friends over

Verbal punishment

If you see your child raise his hands to his sibling, do not hit him in response. Use words, not physical methods, as a punishment for displays of aggression. A verbal reprimand is more effective than a thump.

Expressing aggression

Remember that virtually all children feel angry towards their brothers and sisters sometimes – yet you can insist that hitting is not allowed under any circumstances. Explain the practical effects of physical aggression, for instance: 'When you slap your brother, it hurts him.'

to play, perhaps you can arrange for him to be at his own friend's house at these times.

- If you and your partner dispute the way your children should be managed when they bicker with each other, keep these discussions away from your children's ears. Apart from becoming distressed at watching you disagree, they may take this is an opportunity to do what they want.

Left Make it clear to your child that physical aggression is not acceptable. Stay calm and then drop the subject so that she does not think that hitting her brother is a way of getting attention.

There's too much going on

The arrival of a new baby – and the presence of a growing infant at home – can affect your older child's ability to concentrate. There is so much more going on at home now. With the new family structure, distractions increase and established routines become disrupted.

Above *Keeping your child company when she is playing will help her to concentrate for longer.*

There are several reasons why your older child may find it difficult to concentrate, including:

- Insecurity and jealousy that new arrival is more important.
- Disruption to the family's existing routines.
- The noise of the baby screaming at unpredictable hours.

At times, your child aged 3 or 4 years might be unable to settle at any activity, moving from one game or toy to another without completing any. Likewise, she may appear unsettled and restless when watching a video tape or television programme, whereas before her brother was born she was much more relaxed.

Alternatively, you may find that your pre-schooler doesn't hear you when you ask her to tidy her room or to take her dirty cup into the kitchen. It's hard to know whether she isn't concentrating hard enough or is simply 'tuning out' something she doesn't want to hear – children are very good at that! Either way, however, you can help her to restore her levels of concentration so that she becomes more focused.

Top tips

Be sympathetic

This is the most positive step you can take to boost her attention span. Your child dislikes being unsettled as much as you do – tell her that you can see she is restless and that you want to help her become more relaxed.

Do what you can to eliminate distractions

Background noise distracts her, and also draws her attention in too many different directions at once. Although you can't switch your baby's crying on and off at the touch of a button, you can reduce other background sounds – for instance, by muting the volume on the television set.

Consider potential physical factors

For instance, perhaps she adopts an uncomfortable sitting position, or needs a booster cushion to reach the table when drawing. Remember that a hungry child does not concentrate well, nor does a tired child. Sometimes a brief run around the garden to let off steam may be all that she needs before settling down to concentrate.

Whenever possible, sit beside your child while she plays, reads or watches television

Your physical presence by itself has a very settling effect – there is evidence from psychological research that a young child plays longer with a toy when one of her parents sits beside her.

Boosting self-confidence

The attention shown to your new baby can easily dent your older child's confidence, especially when he is at the pre-school stage. His self-esteem remains vulnerable and he may feel threatened by his younger sibling's presence.

Above *Major milestones, such as riding a bicycle without stabilizers for the first time, should be rewarded with lots of praise – make sure your child knows that you're very proud of her.*

Did you know that...?

- Your pre-school child needs to feel good about himself; he needs to like and value himself – if he doesn't, he will be thoroughly miserable and lack confidence.
- Although a toddler's self-confidence is usually high, the situation often changes at the pre-school stage. His confidence often takes a dip as he begins to compare himself to others his own age.
- The arrival of a new baby in the family can also weaken a 4-year-old's self-confidence, because he is afraid that now he has to compete for attention from his parents.
- Compared to a toddler, a pre-schooler is much more willing to accept the blame for the consequences of his actions. However, this also means that he becomes more aware of his weaknesses and mistakes.
- A child this age is typically very concerned about failure, and is easily troubled when things don't go according to plan. Girls tend to be more self-critical than boys.
- Starting school can result in another dip in your pre-schooler's self confidence. Again, he will compare himself to others his own age, and may suddenly view himself less favourably.

Top tips

Show an interest

Your child wants to share his experiences with you. He also wants you to help him when he has a problem that needs to be resolved. He won't value himself unless he feels valued by you. Make time for him.

Provide a range of activities

Young children are notoriously fickle. However, his self-esteem will stay high if he finds something he is good at, be it sport, dance, art or some other activity.

Praise effort, not outcome

It is very easy for a child to concentrate only on what he achieves or doesn't achieve, so do what you can to encourage him to focus on the process that led to these outcomes. Value his effort, not just the result.

Tell him how much you like him

No matter what age your child is, he loves hearing that you think he is terrific – and he is. His relationship with you has a big influence on his self-confidence, so use this to good effect.

Never compare him to his younger sibling

His confidence will not improve by having it repeatedly pointed out that, for instance, his younger brother has a more pleasant nature than him.

Above Show lots of interest when your child tells you what she's been doing while you weren't there.

new baby and school-age child

- Why routine matters

- Common complaints

- Encouraging kindness

- The critical parent:
  questions and answers

- Fairness, not equality

- The special needs baby

Why routine matters

The most serious challenge a new baby poses to your school-age child is that her established routines may be broken by her young sibling. After all, you have to reorganize your life around the new arrival and therefore it is only reasonable to expect that others in your family (including your older child) will have to make changes, too.

Right *Involve your school-age child in packing her bag and lunchbox. Giving her simple choices like this will help her to feel in control.*

Top tips

Minimize disruption

Once your new baby is home safe and sound, do your best to make sure that your older child's life after school hours is not greatly disrupted. She should still attend all the classes that she did before.

Share the load

Double up with a friend – or group of friends – so that you each take turns ferrying the children back and forward from school. This reduces the number of times you have be involved.

Give her space and responsibility

Let your school-age child organize herself and her timetable so that she can still complete her homework without interruptions. She needs a space in which to work where there are no distractions, even though your house is more crowded now.

Encourage her to maintain existing friendships

She may feel slightly inhibited about bringing friends to the house because of the baby, so give her encouragement and help her plan activities when friends visit.

Changes to routine can, however, have an unsettling effect on her, for the following reasons:

- **Organization.** Most school pupils like to know, for example, that they go to drama class on a Tuesday after school, to swimming lessons at the weekend, and so on. This type of structure enables your child to plan ahead and organize her life.
- **Stability**. She likes her world to operate like clockwork; she has an underlying need for stability. In the same way that unexpected events make you feel momentarily insecure, an unstructured pattern to the day unsettles your older child.
- **Control.** Your child wants to be in control of her life. She's only young, but at this age she still wants to be firmly in the driving seat. Her knowledge that there are daily routines which follow a familiar pattern satisfies this need.
- **Fixed ideas.** Most children are not very adaptable to sudden changes. Flexibility usually improves as she gets older, as her confidence grows. In the meantime, though, she likes things to stay just the way they are.

Right It is important to provide a school-age child with a peaceful environment in which to do her homework.

Common complaints

School-age children commonly express a number of complaints about their younger siblings. Here are some suggestions for dealing with these when they arise.

Above *Spending time with friends is one of the ways in which a child develops her individuality.*

Complaint 'She doesn't do anything all day except eat, cry and make a mess of herself.'

Suggested response Explain to your school-age child that he was once that age, too, and that he should be more patient with his baby sister. You should also let him know that young babies can see and hear more than people generally think they can. For instance, she will soon be able to recognize his face, his voice and even his smell when he holds her.

Complaint 'I'm embarrassed to invite my friends over because I can never have any peace and quiet with them.'

Suggested response Encourage your older child to organize his room carefully so that there is plenty of space for his friends to sit and play together comfortably. Also suggest that he plans the activities before they arrive. And tell him you will help him to have good time by keeping his younger sibling away from him and his pals.

Complaint 'It's no fun going out because it takes you such a long time to get her ready.'

Suggested response Tell him that you enjoy his company and that you really want him to come with you on those short family outings. In addition, ask him to help you with the preparations. Perhaps he can help dress the baby in her outdoor clothes or put all the babycare equipment together in the large carrier bag. He needs to feel involved.

Complaint 'Since the baby has been here, you shout at me all the time.'

Suggested response Resist your instinctive defensive response and consider his comments seriously. Maybe he is just being self-centred, but he may have a point. Your older child is mature enough to notice that you are stressed and a bit more irritable than usual. Stop what you are doing, give him a big hug and reassure him that life will soon get back to normal.

Complaint 'I don't know how to play with her.'

Suggested response Your child may be unsure of how to interact with his young sibling, possibly because he thinks she is fragile and easily upset, or possibly because he simply doesn't realize how to stimulate her. Explain to your older child that the baby will be delighted with anything he does as long as his actions are gentle, caring and steady. He could read to her or slowly wave her rattle in front of her.

Above *Don't take out your tiredness and frustration on your older child, and remember that she needs affection sometimes, too.*

Encouraging kindness

Whereas you had to positively encourage your toddler to care for the new baby because she probably felt threatened by the new arrival, your school-age child has no such sense of insecurity. But you still need to encourage her to care all the same.

Right Talk to your older child, try to get her to feel involved with the baby, and praise her for any help or care she gives.

The danger is that she is so concerned with her own life, pals and leisure pursuits that she only pays cursory attention to her younger sibling. While that minimizes rivalry, it does nothing to develop a close connection between them. So you do need to make the effort to get your school-age child to act caringly towards the new baby.

Discussion

Talk to your older child about your baby's feelings. Explain that he needs to be loved and valued, that he needs to feel part of your family. Research has shown that when a mother takes this approach with their older child, the child is more likely to show affection and concern towards her young sibling; she is also more likely to offer to help with babycare procedures. So have that discussion.

Reinforcement

When she does play positively with the new arrival – even if only for a few moments – give her lots of praise and encouragement. Do the same if she gently cuddles the baby or shows any interest at all. Let her know how pleased you are that she has shown kindness. Your positive reaction reinforces her caring behaviour, making it more likely to be repeated in the future.

Consequences

In addition, point out the good effect that this has on the baby. It helps if you spell out the impact of her caring actions, as they may not be immediately obvious to her. For instance, explain that her baby brother feels happier when he gets loving attention from his big sister; mention that he will reciprocate kindness towards her when he himself is older.

Opinion

Ask your older child's opinion about matters to do with the baby. Instead of getting her involved only on a practical level (as you would do if she was a toddler), seek her thoughts on, say, what toy to buy the baby, what music to play to settle him, or what story to read to him at night. She'll be proud to be asked. Listen to her reply so that she knows you take her seriously.

The critical parent:
questions and answers

Above *How you tell a child off is as important as why – never make criticism seem like a personal attack, but explain that it's a particular piece of behaviour you don't like.*

Q Why is it that my older child annoys me so much? I wait for him to come home from school, but I find myself constantly criticizing him when he does.

A There are a number of factors that make you feel stressed. First, you are tired from caring for your new baby all day. Second, you still have responsibility for ensuring that your school-age child does his homework and so on. And finally, your older child's desire for independence shows through so he may be less cooperative.

Q When I tell him off for making such a mess or for not helping, he ignores me. Why does he do this?

A You criticize him so much – even though you don't mean to – that he has stopped listening. He switches to auto-pilot when you start to complain. Even innocent comments from you become interpreted as complaints, so that you and he are constantly on edge with each other. It is time to change to a more positive approach.

Q Why doesn't he try to sort things out when we have a fight?

A Although you are fed up by the time he gets home, it's up to you sort out disagreements. You can't leave it all to him. Don't let arguments between you and your school-age child stretch from one day into the next, without resolution. Fights rarely die out when left alone – they usually escalate. Do your best to resolve the situation.

Q Is there anything else I can do to make things better between us?

A Tell your child what you like about him, not just what you dislike. A confrontational child will drive any parent to distraction and before you know it, you end up telling him all the horrible things he does. No matter how irritating and uncooperative he is at times, make a conscious effort to point out his good characteristics, too. Try to make a positive comment every day.

Q Does this mean I should never criticize my child?

A There is always a place for 'gentle criticism', which involves saying something positive at the same time. For instance, instead of becoming irritated because he didn't help you bath his young sibling, you could say 'I'm surprised you didn't help me with bathing the baby because you are normally so helpful.' This encourages your child to see how he can be more responsive the next time and avoids another argument.

Below Too much criticism without the balance of praise will make any child unhappy and uncooperative.

Fairness, not equality

Fairness is more appropriate than equality because it means responding to each of your children's distinctive and individual preferences, skills, characteristics and talents. Treating them fairly makes each of them feel special.

Left Treating your children fairly, and considering their respective needs, will help to ensure that they get on together.

Here are some of the typical sibling rivalry conflicts you may have to deal with:

- Your older child moans that when she was her younger brother's age, she wasn't allowed to stay up so late.
- Your younger child is aggrieved because his older sister is allowed to choose which television programme to watch and he isn't given that responsibility.
- Both your children are totally convinced that the other's share of the sweets is bigger than their own, even though they have the same amount.
- Your older child comments that she was never allowed to be as cheeky as her brother when she was that age.

The temptation is then to match each child exactly with the other, stage by stage, hour by hour, sweet by sweet, activity by activity, in the hope that by treating them equally (giving each exactly same as the other), peace and quiet will reign in your house once more. You would think that logically this is a good solution – but it rarely works. After all, why should they both, for instance, have to eat the same type and amount of sweets when they have different tastes and different appetites?

Aim for fairness instead. That's a much more sensible parenting goal, because it means that each of your children is more likely to get what they want. For example, suppose both your children have musical talent. They don't have to learn to play the same musical instrument in order to make them feel they are being treated even-handedly. That would be an ineffective strategy if one child would prefer to play the clarinet while the other was interested in the piano.

Is she justified?

There may be times when one of your children insists that she is treated neither fairly nor equally in comparison to her younger sibling. Hear what she has to say and consider her argument very carefully. If you think there is no case to answer, tell her so. But if you think she has a point, be honest enough to tell her that, too. Then do what you can to make the situation better.

The special needs baby

If your new baby has special needs, your school-age child is smart enough to be aware of this. He'll know there is a problem, so don't keep him in the dark. Explain his young sibling's special needs to him as best you can, using age-appropriate language and without giving him too much information to digest.

Above Making time for your other children is especially important when you have a special needs baby.

Of course, your baby with special needs probably requires more attention than your other child, perhaps because she is more dependent on you for longer or because you have so many different hospital appointments. It's never easy balancing these demands on your time and attention so that your other children don't feel left out.

Pressures

Psychologists have found four main pressures on siblings of children with special needs. Here are some strategies to help you cope with them:

Excessive responsibility You may fall into the trap of asking your other child to do much more to help around the house than would normally be expected, because you are so busy looking after your baby with special needs.

Strategy By all means enlist his help with domestic chores – that's part of normal family life – but don't overburden him with tasks.

Sense of abandonment Your older child might start to feel he matters less than his sibling with special needs, because you are so preoccupied with her care. He knows he shouldn't feel this way but he just can't help himself.

Strategy Tell you older child that you guess he feels left out at times because of the baby and that you'll make it up to him by, say, just the two of you going out at the weekend.

Unrealistic goals True, in comparison with your baby who has special needs, your older child is very fortunate. But that doesn't mean he has to be perfect in every way, that he has to achieve at the highest level and be the best behaved child ever. Such a goal is unrealistic.

Strategy Accept each child as an individual. Encourage him to develop his potential to the full without setting unattainable targets for him.

Excessive reliance In some instances, a child with special needs remains dependent on very basic parental support much longer than would normally be expected. The other sibling can begin to resent this because, for instance, it limits family outings.

Strategy The more he understands his sibling's difficulties, the less he'll resent her. It is also worth pointing out that he is still dependent on you at times, too.

Above A special needs baby will need extra time and attention but it is important not to treat him too differently from your other children.

as they get older

- When the age gap is small

- When the age gap is large

- Ages and stages (6 to 14 years)

- Avoiding comparisons

- Resolving disputes

- Older siblings: *questions and answers*

When the age gap is small

When the age gap is small (say, between 1 and 2 years) and both your children are older, the dynamics of their relationships change. There are both advantages and disadvantages to this situation.

Pros

- They can go out together – their closeness in age means that it is socially acceptable for each to be seen in the other's company.
- They can share friends – there are many instances where two siblings are in the same circle of friends.
- There is a good chance they can become very close pals – this commonality acts as a glue that keeps them together.

Cons

- They may compete with each other – being so close in age, the competitive factor can easily intensify during adolescence.
- They may feel stifled by each other – their closeness in age might mean that they feel they can't ever get away from their sibling.
- They may resent each other – the older one might feel that she is always expected to be responsible for her younger sibling when they are out.

Right If your younger child has someone of their own age to play with, the older children are less likely to feel that they are being imposed on.

Left Mix responsibility and freedom: encourage your older child to play with her younger brother; but also allow her time with her own friends.

The positive view

Always try to emphasize the advantages and minimize the disadvantages. Use the strengths of their small age gap as your children grow older: encourage them to be friends, to listen to each other and to share their ideas with each other. For instance, your older child's school experience can be extremely helpful to her younger sibling, who is perhaps only a year behind her in the education system – she can use this knowledge to help prepare her younger brother or sister for the transfer to secondary school.

Give them more responsibility for resolving their differences. Don't jump in immediately when they start to disagree, as you might have done when they were younger. Instead, let them take ownership of their conflict. Children older than 6 should be able to sort out most things by themselves.

Drifting apart

No matter how strong their relationship, points will arise when they drift apart because they are temporarily in different developmental phases – for example, when the youngest is 10 or 11 years old and the older one is 13 or 14 with a new interest in opposite-gender relationships, or when the older one has left school while the younger one remains fully immersed in that stage of education. Don't worry about these temporary episodes. Your children will draw closer together again once they are back in the same phase of development.

When the age gap is large

When the age gap is large (say, 6 or 7 years and more), the sibling relationship still changes as the children grow older. However, the tendency for the older child to be kindly and paternalistic to his younger sibling typically remains constant. This is especially true when the age gap stretches into double figures; in this instance, the younger child might view his older sibling more as an uncle or aunt than as a brother or sister.

Below *Sibling rivalry is much less likely to occur when there is a large age gap between siblings.*

One of the plus points of a large age gap is that jealousy is usually non-existent because your children's stages of development are so far apart. On the contrary: their relationship is usually hallmarked by genuine concern for and interest in each other. The drawback, of course, is that they are so far apart in age that they cannot establish the sort of sharing friendship which often develops when there is a small age gap.

Potential problems

When there is a large age gap, your children may experience two unsettling trends as they grow older:

Your younger child continues to see himself as 'the youngest'

You would expect each of your children to assume increasing responsibility for themselves as they grow older – this is part of the maturation process. Where the age gap between siblings is large, there can be a tendency for the younger child to continue to view himself as a more dependent, very young child, even when he has reached older childhood and adolescence. 'Being the youngest' becomes

the way he defines himself. Try to ensure, therefore, that he steadily improves his independence and that he does not constantly rest under the protection of his older sibling.

Your older child struggles to accept your youngest growing up

Of course age gap remains constant as your children grow, but the children themselves obviously mature. However, you may find that your older child constantly sees her younger sibling as 'the baby' of the family, and consequently fails to take his problems, challenges and attainments seriously. This can create tension, if your younger child resents the fact that his older sister trivializes his difficulties. You may need to work hard to ensure that your older child gives full respect to her younger sibling as they grow older.

Sorting out these potential hazards goes a long way towards enabling your children to develop a long-lasting, positive sibling relationship which survives not just through childhood but throughout adulthood as well.

Above *As she grows up, the 'baby of the family' may need encouragement to become more independent.*

85

Ages and stages (6 to 14 years)

Relationships between siblings continue to change as they grow older. The school years provide new challenges and new experiences which influence the way in which brothers and sisters interact with each other.

6 years

Your school-age child's friendships increase in significance, although these can change from one day to the next. She wants to be liked and to be included.

She is the older child

She may find her younger sibling irritating and constantly complains that he annoys her intensely. She likes to boss him about.

She is the younger child

She now begins to understand the meaning of respect and privacy. She speaks up for herself when she thinks something is unfair.

7 and 8 years

Many children become more confident and outgoing at this age; experience in school increases her self-belief. She becomes more assertive.

She is the older child

She takes her responsibility for her younger sibling seriously, especially if they attend the same school. At times, though, she likes to be on her own.

She is the younger child

She looks to her older sibling for help and advice, and she is proud of any achievements he makes.

9 and 10 years

Self-image is vulnerable at this age. Physical appearance matters, and all it takes is a simple negative comment about her clothes to reduce her to tears.

She is the older child
Her younger sibling's misbehaviour annoys her, yet she'll defend him fiercely when she sees others treat him unfairly.

She is the younger child
She wants to mix socially with her older sibling and his friends, and perhaps take part in the same leisure activities.

11 and 12 years

The influence of the peer group starts to dominate now, and she wants to be like them rather than like others in her family.

She is the older child
Relationships with younger siblings can become strained at this stage, as she tries to develop a distinctive identity for herself and her friends.

She is the younger child
Admiration of older siblings may diminish temporarily. She wants to make up her own mind about things and prefers to talk to her friends about things which matter to her.

13 and 14 years

Opposite-gender relationships start to attract her attention. She is also more able to cope with complex and abstract ideas.

She is the older child
Your adolescent feels significantly more mature than her younger sibling. She may become rather patronizing towards him.

She is the younger child
The older sibling is often seen as a rich source of advice on managing opposite-gender relationships.

Avoiding comparisons

Do your best to resist comparing one of your children with an other – it will always make at least one of them totally miserable.

Above *Each child needs to develop their own interests and to be praised on their own merits.*

Problem When you tell your younger child that he is not as tidy as his older sister, he flies into a rage and then sulks.

Solution Comparison with his older sibling has a negative effect because he does not want her to be used as a benchmark for his behaviour. Try using other reasons to encourage him to be tidy – he'll be able to find his toys more easily, or his clothes won't be crumpled when he puts them on, for example.

Problem Your older child makes fun of his younger sister's school achievements, telling you he did much more when he was that age.

Solution This type of comparison devalues the importance of your younger child's achievements. Explain to your older child that he and his sibling are different children, with different talents and abilities. What matters is they do their best. Encourage him to take pride in anything his sister achieves, just as she would with him.

Problem Your youngest child's school teacher regularly compares him to his older sister.

Solution Speak to the teacher as soon as you realize this comparison is being made. Emphasize that you want each of your children to be treated individually and that that you are concerned that your younger child may feel undervalued. Suggest tactfully that his progress should be evaluated against himself, not against his older sister.

Problem Although you never compare your children, your younger child spontaneously compares himself to his older sibling all the time.

Solution Let your younger child know that you value him for the terrific child he is, not for how well he compares to his sister (or to anyone else, for that matter). He needs to accept and judge himself by his own standards. Your comments may be all that is required for him to cease these comparisons.

Problem Both your children want to join in the same activity, and you are concerned that their differing abilities could create tension between them.

Solution Find a way to indulge their similar interest but without allowing unhelpful competition. For instance, if they both want to play sport, lead each of them towards a different game and find them different coaches and/or teams. This type of strategy is rarely convenient for parents, but it's certainly worth the effort in the long run.

Above Children are naturally competitive and may see being better at something than their siblings as a way of getting attention. Try to discourage this sort of comparison.

Resolving disputes

As your children grow older, the chances are that there still will be moments – or longer periods – when tension arises between them. This is perfectly normal, occurring even in positive sibling relationships. However, research shows that physical aggression (for example, hitting, kicking or biting) between siblings diminishes with age, and negative emotions are more likely to be expressed verbally.

'I had hoped they would stop fighting since they are both older and more mature. It is true to say they bicker less, but they still have some serious fights. Sometimes they don't talk to each other for days.'

Richard, father of Rebecca (9) and Dean (7)

The way you manage arguments between your children should also change now that your children are beyond those early pre-school years. As they have grown older, you will have adapted your approach to their increased understanding, experience and ability.

Remain positive

Although you may feel pessimistic because your children still bicker despite their age and maturity, keep reminding yourself that the situation will improve. Try to keep an upbeat perspective and remember that it is only natural for siblings to have disagreements. When you think about it, you'll realize they do actually fight less than they did when they were younger.

Step back

Be prepared to play a neutral role at first when they disagree with each other. Beyond the pre-school years, your children have learned skills to help resolve conflict with their siblings. They need to be given room to practise these skills within their relationship without your intervention.

Above *It is better to encourage older children to resolve their own disputes and come up with their own solutions rather than impose yours on them.*

Give them responsibility

Older children can often be successful at sorting out disputes mainly on their own, but may occasionally need some support from their parents. Insist that they sit down together to talk about the area of conflict. Sit with them as well, but don't dominate. By all means give occasional prompts to stimulate discussion, but that's all.

Don't let disputes last

Ironically, the older your children are, the less likely their disagreements are to be resolved within minutes – this happens because conflicts now tend to be over more serious matters. If they are in dispute for more than a couple of hours, help them sort it out without taking over entirely.

Moving on

Once their argument is over, encourage your children to reach an agreement on how such tension can be avoided in the future. They should agree on a common strategy that suits both of them. Give them lots of praise for resolving this conflict maturely, and then let the matter drop.

Older siblings:
questions and answers

Right *Although siblings are likely to have very different interests, spending time together as they grow older will help to keep their relationship strong.*

Q Isn't it the case that siblings get on better when they are older anyway, and that any previous grudges and tensions spontaneously disappear?

A Not necessarily. All that happens is that if siblings have unresolved negative feelings stemming from childhood, they simply learn to control these feelings more effectively when they are older. Tensions need to be sorted out early on otherwise they are likely to emerge later.

Q Should we still have family outings now that the children are older, with widely different interests?

A Yes, you should. Family outings provide a great opportunity for you to strengthen the children's relationship with each other. The very act of deciding where to go is a useful mechanism for encouraging them to think about each other's wishes and for increasing their sensitivity.

Q My children prefer to eat their evening meal while watching television. Is there anything wrong with that?

A Having a meal while watching television can be a wonderful treat, but it is best that this practice does not become a regular part of their routine. Sibling relationships need good communication, and there is more opportunity for constructive dialogue to take place when you and your family share a meal together than when you each stare silently at the television screen.

Q What else can I do to keep their relationship strong when they are older?

A Continue to emphasize the value and self-worth of their sibling. For instance, encourage them to praise each other's achievements, whether that involves watching each other's performance in the school play or congratulating each other on exam successes. Perhaps suggest that they choose each other thoughtful presents on special occasions (and that they contribute some of their pocket money towards their purchase).

Q Can siblings really be friends when they are adolescents and then adults?

A Of course they can. Siblings have the possibility of a very special relationship – after all, no other friend spends so much time in their company, shares so many experiences with them, or knows them for so long. If your children learn to love and care for each other during childhood, this positive relationship could remain strong throughout the rest of their lives.

Index

Acknowledgements

Bubbles/David Robinson 92
Family Life Picture Library/Angela Hampton 91
Octopus Publishing Group Limited/Peter
   Pugh-Cook 1, 2, 5, 6, 7, 8, 10, 11, 12,
   13, 14, 15, 16, 17, 18, 20, 21, 22, 23,
   24, 25, 26, 27, 28, 30, 31, 32, 33, 34,
   35, 36, 37, 38, 40, 42, 43, 44, 45, 46,
   47, 48, 49, 50, 51, 52, 55, 56, 57, 58,
   59, 60, 61, 62, 64, 65, 66, 68, 69, 70,
   71, 72, 74, 75, 76, 78, 79, 80, 82, 83,
   84, 85, 88, 89
Photodisc 86

Executive editor: Jane McIntosh
Editor: Rachel Lawrence
Senior designer: Joanna Bennett
Designer: Ginny Zeal
Production controller: Edward Carter